Carving an 1880s Western Train
Its Passengers & Crew

Caricature Carvers of America

Schiffer Publishing Ltd®
4880 Lower Valley Road · Atglen, PA · 19310

Designed by RoS
Type set in Zurich BT

ISBN: 978-0-7643-3381-1
Printed in China

Schiffer Books are available at special discounts for bulk purchases for sales promotions or premiums. Special editions, including personalized covers, corporate imprints, and excerpts can be created in large quantities for special needs. For more information contact the publisher:

Published by Schiffer Publishing Ltd.
4880 Lower Valley Road
Atglen, PA 19310
Phone: (610) 593-1777; Fax: (610) 593-2002
E-mail: Info@schifferbooks.com

For the largest selection of fine reference books on this and related subjects, please visit our web site at www.schifferbooks.com
We are always looking for people to write books on new and related subjects. If you have an idea for a book please contact us at the above address.

This book may be purchased from the publisher.
Include $5.00 for shipping.
Please try your bookstore first.
You may write for a free catalog.

In Europe, Schiffer books are distributed by
Bushwood Books
6 Marksbury Ave.
Kew Gardens
Surrey TW9 4JF England
Phone: 44 (0) 20 8392 8585; Fax: 44 (0) 20 8392 9876
E-mail: info@bushwoodbooks.co.uk
Website: www.bushwoodbooks.co.uk

Contents

Dedication

This book is dedicated to the memory of the five deceased members of the Caricature Carvers of America: Claude Bolton, Dave Dunham, Tex Hasse, Dave Rasmussen, and Joe Wannamaker. They were instrumental in the development of the CCA during our formative years. Their contributions to the art of caricature carving are immeasurable.

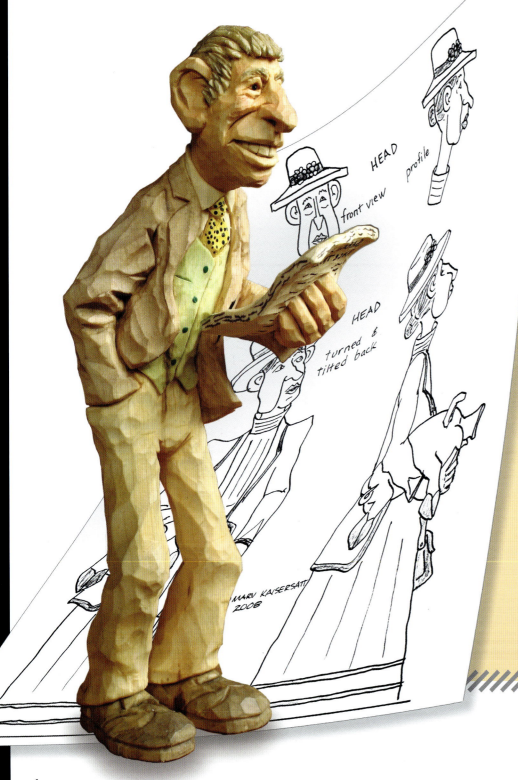

Active members 2008
Vicki Bishop
David Boone
Tom Brown
P.J. Dricoll
Gary Falin
Gene Fuller
Bruce Henn
Eldon Humphreys
Marv Kaisersatt
Randy Landen
Pete LeClair
Keith Morrill
Steve Prescott
Doug Raine
Floyd Rhadigan
David Sabol
Joe Schumacher
Dave Stetson
Dennis Thornton
Bob Travis
Jack A. Williams
Tom Wolfe
Joe You

Emeritus members
Gary Batte
Phil Bishop
Harold Enlow
Desiree Hajny
Will Hayden
Peter Ortel
Vic Otto
Jack Price
Harley Refsal
Harley Schmitgen
Gerald Sears
Cleve Taylor
Rich Wetherbee

Deceased members
Claude Bolton
Dave Dunham
Tex Haase
Dave Rasmussen
Joe Wannamaker

Introduction

As this book is being published the Caricature Carvers of America (CCA) will be approaching their 20th anniversary. It hardly seems possible that nearly 20 years ago, November 1990 to be exact, ten of the founding members met for the first time in the back room of Paxton Lumber Company in Fort Worth, Texas, to discuss the concept of forming a national organization to promote caricature carving. The feeling among those present was that caricature carving needed the glare of publicity to draw attention to its creativity and expand its acceptance in the art world. The Caricature Carvers of America was formed with those concepts in mind.

The first order of business was to develop a mission for the new organization. The founding ten who attended that meeting unanimously agreed that the primary objective of the CCA would be to promote the art of caricature carving. How to best accomplish that objective was unclear at that time. The new organization considered carving projects, seminars, exhibits, and books, but ultimately, the CCA's approach to promoting caricature carving would develop over the next few years.

The second topic of discussion for the newly formed organization was membership. Experience suggested that full membership participation in any project would be critical to our success. From a practical perspective we established membership at 25, in the belief that a larger membership would make full participation on group projects prohibitive.

Looking back over the past 20 years we have much to celebrate. This project marks our fourth book on caricature carving in paperback, and a fifth is available in CD format on our web site. The *Full Moon Saloon* and *Carving the CCA Circus*, our first books, have become standards in the world of caricature carving. *Caricature Carvers Showcase*, published in 2007 is already in its second printing. We have worked diligently to provide a variety of exhibits around the country, in an effort to expose people to caricature carving. And, our members teach literally hundreds of seminars each year. Seven years ago we initiated the National Caricature Carving competition. The competition, open to all caricature carvers, encourages creativity and originality through a nationally recognized competition. The annual event has become highly successful and, while not part of the original plan, has been a source for several of our newest members. In addition, we sponsor a CCA merit ribbon program for woodcarving shows throughout the US. Winners are entered into a CCA national registry.

So, the question remains…have we been successful in helping to promote the art of caricature carving? Peruse the latest issue of *Chip Chats* and other carving magazines and look at photographs of the CCA's National Caricature Carving Competition or the International Woodcarvers Congress. If we have had even a modest part in encouraging caricature carvers, then we believe the answer is yes. But ultimately, we'll let you be the judge.

Our active membership, while limited to 25 at any given time, has included 39 caricature carvers over the past 20 years. Many of them are widely recognized in the field of caricature carving. They are the people who are responsible for seeing that the CCA meets its principle objective, now and into the future. Unfortunately, we have lost five of our members. We will not forget Dave Rasmussen's Minnesota farmers, Claude Bolton's Texas cowboys, Tex Hasse's western caricatures, Dave Dunham's unbounded humor so effortlessly expressed in his carvings, or Joe Wannamaker's ability to express life's everyday occurrences in his caricatures. Nor will we forget the contributions that these members made to the art of caricature carving.

Photo by Jack A. and Carole Williams

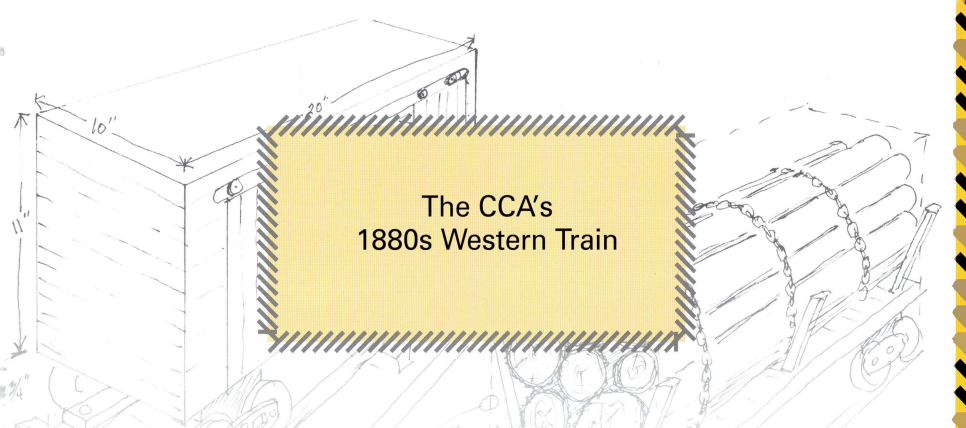

The CCA's 1880s Western Train

Major carving projects are a part of the larger scope of activities the CCA undertakes in its mission to promote the art of caricature carving. The CCA Train was our third major project, following the Full Moon Saloon and the CCA Circus. The train began its journey as a suggestion by Dave Stetson that we carve an 1880s era train, complete with a supporting cast of characters. Dave arrived at the CCA's 2004 annual meeting in Dollywood, Tennessee, well prepared to present his idea to our membership. He brought a caricature box-car on a section of track, complete with hobos, to tangibly illustrate his vision for the project.

His idea was an instant hit with the membership and we voted unanimously to undertake the project. The scale was set at one inch to the foot, and excitement quickly swept through the room as members volunteered to take on major portions of the project.

Once the project was adopted and formalized, we agreed to bring the completed train and supporting carvings to our annual meeting the following year. Thus, when we returned to Dollywood for our 2005 meeting the bulk of the train came with us (except for the log car, which was "misplaced" by the airline, and went missing for several weeks).

The intial set-up, which was a complicated process, came next. Naturally, we placed the engine and tender at the front and the caboose at the end, but the remainder of the layout was a little more challenging. Organized chaos might be an overstatement, but it does accurately describe our efforts to organize the train. Cars were placed where the builders felt they would appear in the train. Collectively, we arranged, re-arranged, and arranged again until we felt the train had balance, and each piece was appropriately displayed. It was a job well done…well, almost done. On careful examination it became clear that we needed more carvings to round out the scene. So, after setting the train up for its debut at Dollywood, we agreed to bring the additional carvings to complete the scene to our next annual meeting. What began as a one-year project ultimately spanned two years. In 2006 we added the final pieces, and the train became the final project you see in this book.

7

Gary Batte
Stephenville, Texas
• hobo with cigar

Phil Bishop
Elk City, Oklahoma
• Dear John
• Coolie

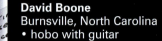

David Boone
Burnsville, North Carolina
• hobo with guitar

Gene Fuller
Boise, Idaho
• Chief Sasquatch

Desiree Hajny
Bule Hill, Nebraska
• owl

Will Hayden
Vancouver, Washington
• conductor Bolton.

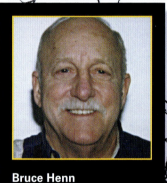

Bruce Henn
Troy, Ohio
• sleeping hobo
• bathtime hobo

Keith Morrill
Custer, South Dakota
• ticket buyer
• man with baggage wagon
• baggage handler

Vic Otto
Boise, Idaho
• log car
• a hooded man on log car

Steve Prescott
Forth Worth, Texas
• oiler
• conductor
• lady and child in passenger car

Doug Raine
Tucson, Arizona
• engine and tender

Floyd Rhadigan
Saline, Michigan
• Indian man
• Indian woman

Tom Brown
Converse, Indiana
• water tower

Harold Enlow
Dogpatch, Arkansas
• old man on caboose.

Gary Falin
Alcoa, Tennessee
• passenger car
• mechanic

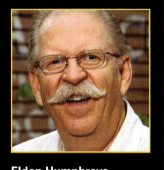

Eldon Humphreys
Guelph, Ontario, Canada
• man sitting in box car
• man in knit cap.

Marv Kaisersatt
Faribault, Minnesota
• cow
• engineer
• lady with pig

Randy Landen
Derby, Kansas
• tagger

Pete LeClair
Gardner, Massachusetts
• depot
• passenger with bag
• preacher
• man with racing form
• ticket agent

David Sabol
Wrightsville, Pennsylvania
• balloon boy

Harley Schmitgen
Blue Earth, Minnesota
• crossing gate

Joe Schumacher
Imperial, Missouri
• hanging caboose man
• Bull, CCA detective

Gerald Sears
Soutwest City, Missouri
• caboose

Dave Stetson
Scottsdale, Arizona
• box car
• man climbing in box car
• man helping man climb in box car

9

"The Merchant"

BY DENNIS THORNTON '06

Cleve Taylor
Boise, Idaho
• log car
• man pulling lever on log car

Dennis Thornton
Guilford, New York
• man pushing cart with chicken
• boxes; barrels; and safe in depot

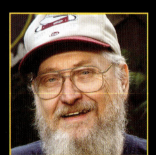

Bob Travis
Davis, California
• robbery scene

Jack A. Williams
Sun City West, Arizona
• passenger car

Tom Wolfe
Spruce Pine, North Carolina
• hand car
• two guys in hand car
• cat on hand car
• dog chasing hand car.

Joe You
Sacramento, California
• "Karv Maisersatt," carver
• two dogs watching carver

BUILDING THE CCA TRAIN

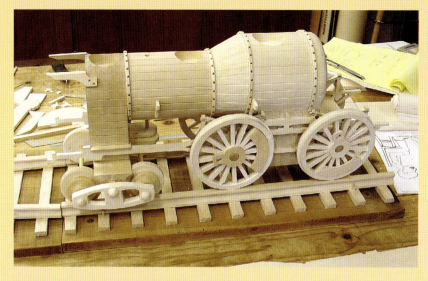

The Engine & Tender: Doug Raine, photos by Robert Raine

When the proposal to build an 1880s train and to carve supporting caricature figures was accepted we all immediately began thinking of possible contributions we might make to the overall scene. However, after a brief discussion it soon became apparent that the most difficult and time consuming task would be the construction of the engine and train cars. Dave Stetson had completed the box car for use in presenting the proposal to the group. He also prepared specifications for wheel size, truck construction, and track dimensions. At that point all we needed was the rest of the train. Fortunately, several members agreed to handle that part of the project.

Doug Raine immediately volunteered to build the engine and tender. We knew the engine would be the focal point of the project. Doug was an important contributor to our earlier projects so we also knew that the engine and tender were in good hands. We were not disappointed. The following series of photographs follow Doug's progress as the engine comes together.

Other members quickly volunteered to contribute additional cars. As noted earlier Dave Stetson built the box car in preparation for presenting the proposal to our group. So, we were off to a good start. Jack A. Williams and Gary Falin volunteered to build the passenger car. Vic Otto and Cleve Taylor added the log car.

The Passenger Car: Jack A. Williams & Gary Falin; photos by Michele Stetson

The Boxcar: Dave Stetson,
photos by Michelle Stetson

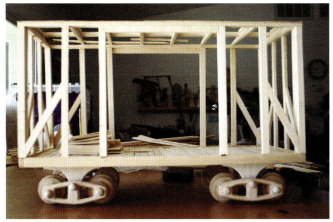

The Log Car: Vic Otto and Cleve Taylor. Construction photos by Vic Otto; finished car photo by Jack A. Williams

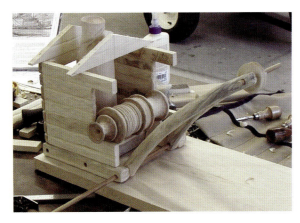

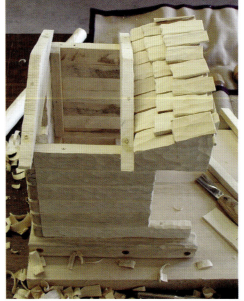

The Caboose: Gerald Sears,
photos by Barbara Sears

Unlike today's trains, no self-respecting train of the 1880s would be without a caboose. Gerald Sears took on that responsibility. Gerald began his research by seeking out a real caboose and compiling a series of reference photographs. He followed this up by designing, and building, the CCA caboose.

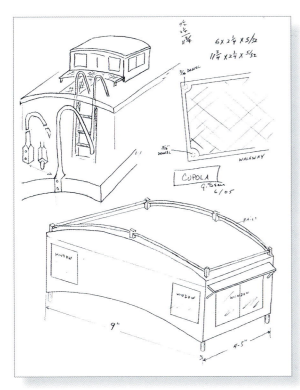

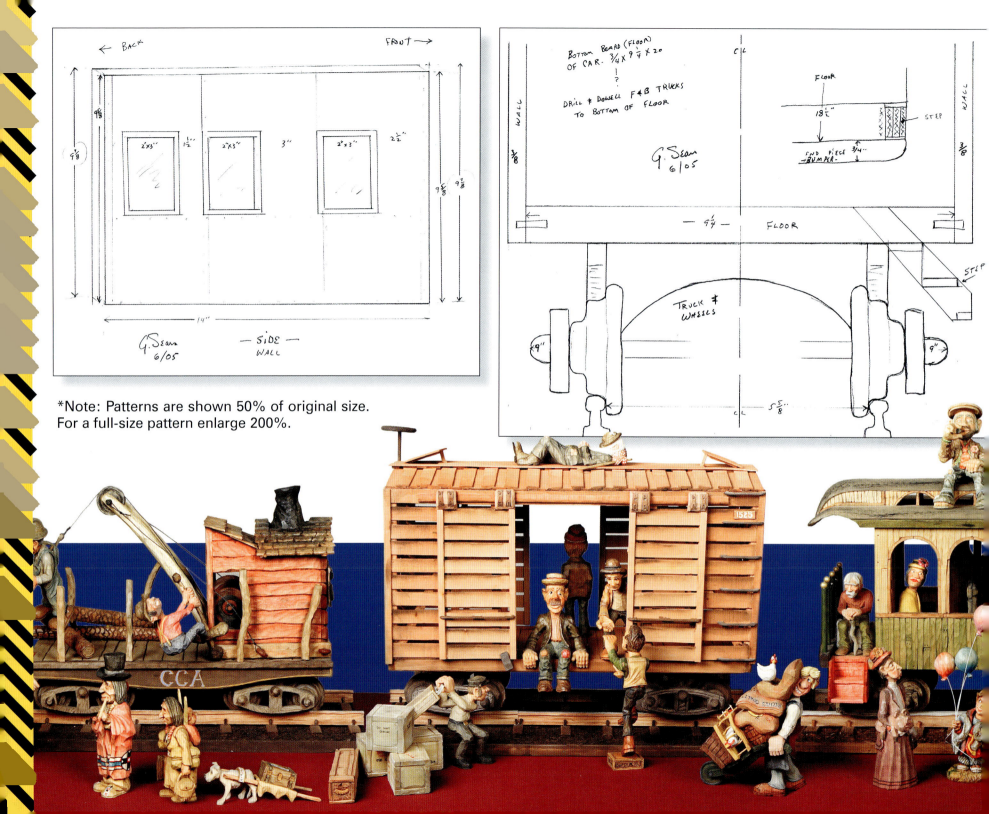

← BACK   FRONT →

9⅝

2"×3"   1½"   2"×3"   3"   2"×3"   2½"

9⅝   9⅞

14"

G. Sears
6/05

— SIDE —
WALL

BOTTOM BOARD (FLOOR)
OF CAR. ¾ × 9¼ × 20
|
?
DRILL & DOWELL F&B TRUCKS
TO BOTTOM OF FLOOR

WALL   C|L   FLOOR

G. Sears
6/05

18½"   STEP

END PIECE ¾"
—BUMPER—

⅜   ⅜

9¼   FLOOR

STEP

TRUCK &
WHEELS

9"   9"

C|L   5⅝

*Note: Patterns are shown 50% of original size.
For a full-size pattern enlarge 200%.

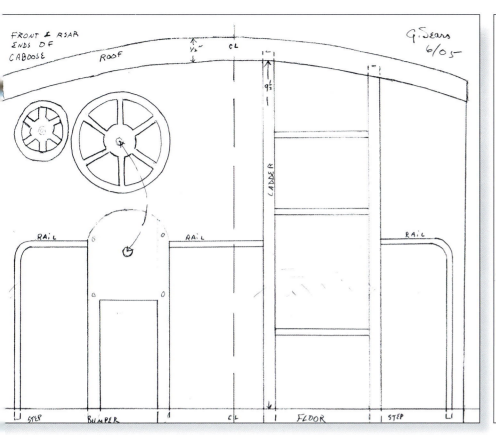

FRONT & REAR ENDS OF CABOOSE

ROOF

CL

9½"

LADDER

RAIL

RAIL

RAIL

STEP

BUMPER

CL

FLOOR

STEP

G. Sears
6/05

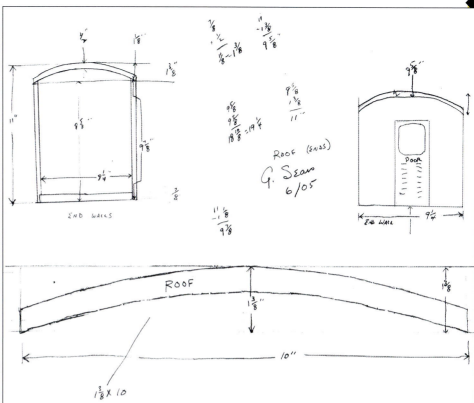

END WALLS

ROOF (ENDS)
G. Sears
6/05

DOOR

END WALL

9½"

ROOF

1⅜"

10"

1⅜ X 10

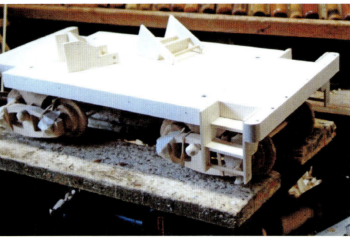

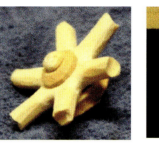

STEP-BY-STEP CARVING INSTRUCTIONS FOR CARVING A CARICATURE FIGURE

Dave Stetson, 2008

One thing that makes the CCA such a unique organization is the diversity of styles offered by the membership. Along with the diverse style offerings, the members use various methods and processes to create their figures. This is but one of the methods used to design and execute a figure. Many members use some of the same methods with differing approaches as suits their particular needs.

This figure is designed to assist another figure who is climbing into the boxcar of the train.

To exaggerate reality, one must know what they are exaggerating. Your hands won't be able to create what isn't in your mind so one must know their subject to create it. Sometimes I start with a drawing or use a manikin armature with clay to work out the pose and detail. In this case, I have used a template that was sized to the other figures to keep them all proportioned the same.

(Photography is courtesy of Michele Stetson, copyright 2008.)

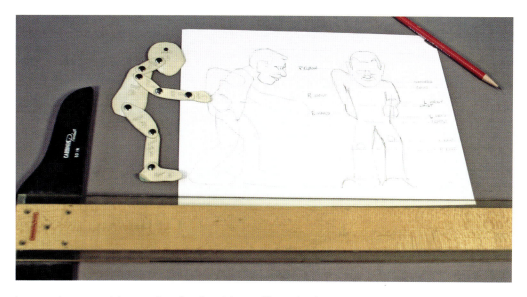

I created a moveable template for the side profile and using a T-square extend key points across the page to layout a front view that will proportionally line up with the side view.

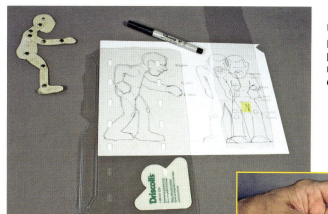

Using recycled mylar or plastic packaging material and a felt pen, I trace the drawing and make a pattern to transfer the drawing to the wood.

Cut out the plastic film with common scissors.

27

The completed operation.

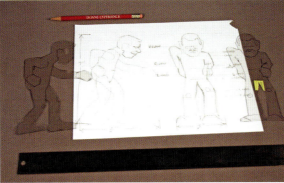

Completed patterns with materials.

Mylar patterns applied to block of wood. Notice a common base line on both sides of the block so the front and side patterns line up.

Another view of patterns on the block of wood.

Showing the completed reattachment with hot melt glue, leaving squared sides to enable cutting of the front profile.

Cut the front profile on the bandsaw.

Final cut of the front profile.

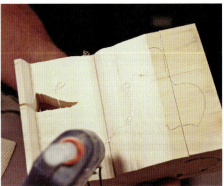

Re-attach waste cuts with hot melt glue to recreate squared sides to enable cutting of the side profile.

Use a screwdriver to pry off glued waste pieces after finishing the side profile cuts.

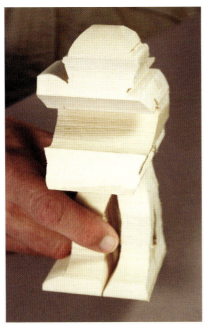

Completed bandsaw cutout.

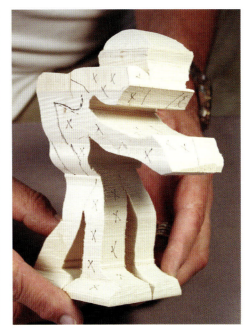

Right front side of bandsaw blank marked with areas to be removed.

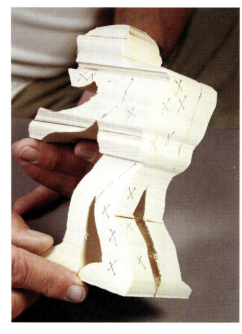

Left rear side of bandsaw blank with areas marked to be removed.

Left front side of bandsaw blank with areas marked to be removed.

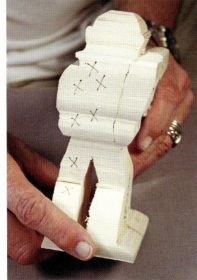

Back side of bandsaw blank with areas marked to be removed.

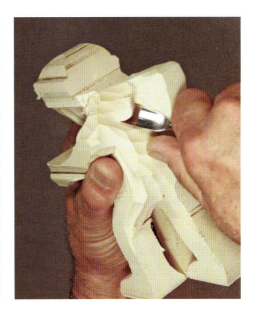

After the extra left rear leg and arm are removed, remove the extra right arm and leg. Use a shallow gouge, 3/4" #5, to remove excess material from the blank.

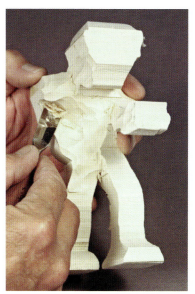

Remove the extra material from the front side of the right arm.

29

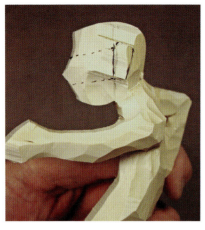

Mark the head with an eye line half way between the top of the head and the bottom of the chin. Then mark the bottom of the nose half way between the eye line and the chin.

Draw a vertical line halfway between the front and the back of the head to represent the front edge of the ear. Extend the eye line and the nose line to the side of the head to represent the attachment point of the top of the ear and the ear lobe. The top flap of the ear lines up with the brow.

Outline the ear and remove excess wood on the sides of the face to leave the ear proud on the head. Mark the hair line and jaw line (the jaw line runs from the bottom of the earlobe to the chin.)

Mark the knees, wrists, and sleeves. Layout the ear.

Undercut the nose and taper the sides of the nose to the eye line. Outline the hair and remove wood from the forehead and sides of the face to leave the hair proud. Make some opening cuts inside the ear. Remove the corners from the arms and hands and gouge around the neck. Remove a chip from inside the ear.

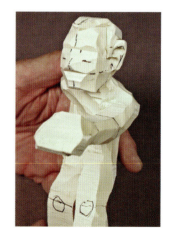
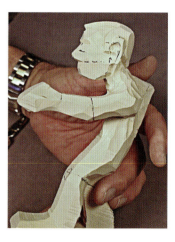

Another view.

Mark reference points on the face, centerline on forehead, nose and chin. Mark the width of the nose on the eye line. Then mark a point between the eye line and the nose line for the cheekbone.

Another view.

View showing ear with 2 gouge cuts blocking in the inside ear cartilage.

Left side view.

Draw a half circle that connects the nose width mark to the cheekbone. This line will represent a proportional mound for the eye.

Using a 2 mm veiner, carve under and inside the marked circle for the eye mound (carve only the lower half of the circle, the upper half will represent the expressive area of the brow).

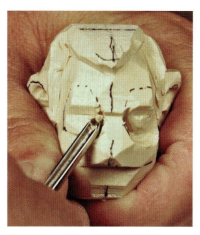

Another view.

View of the completed eye mounds. A knife was used to carve the mound after the veiner outline.

A slicing cut across the cheekbone and under the eye mound...

...rotating the blade upward at the nose, will create the width of the nose.

Mark the outline of the nostrils and the nasal labial fold, and outline the upper and lower eyelids.

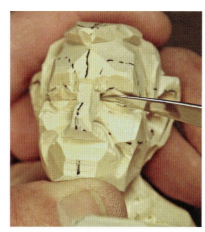

Trim out the eye opening with a knife after using a "V" tool to cut the nostrils and nasal labial fold.

Finishing the eye cut on the left eye.

With the point of the knife, remove a triangular chip from the side of the nostril to set the nostril back into the face.

Prepare the brow for expression by creating a deep cut just above the brow circle with a 5 mm veiner.

Using a knife, trim back the forehead to the hair line to leave the brow proud.

Final trim cuts to the hairline.

Make a shallow gouge cut from the corner of the eye to the sideburns to set the cheek bone shelf.

View of head with the eyes and nose blocked in and the brow and nasal labial fold set for expression.

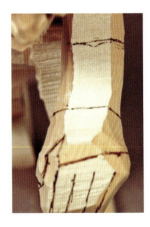    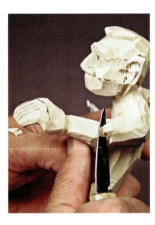

Layout for the left wrist, knuckles, thumb, and fingers.

Layout and trim wood away from bottom of feet.

Trim away the corners of the legs.

Set the shirt sleeve with a "V" tool and set the wrist with a gouge.

Trim the forearm from the wrist to the shirt sleeve.

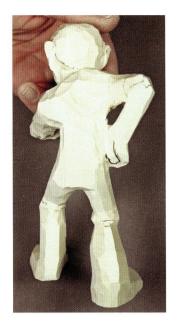

Rear view of carving showing the layout of the palm and little finger on the right hand.

View of right hand showing layout of thumb and fingers. Left hand fingers have been separated with a "V" tool.

Another view.

Left side view of carving blocked in and ready for detail.

Right side view of carving blocked in and ready for detail.

Right rear 3/4 view of carving blocked in and ready for detail.

Cut the upper eyelid fold with a "V" tool and draw in the mouth line.

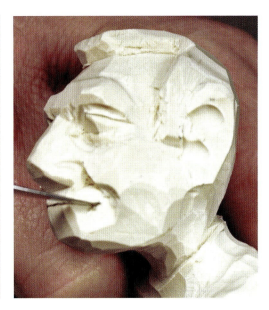

Remove a 3-corner chip from the corner of the mouth along side the lower lip and cut a dividing line between the lips.

Run a 5 mm veiner under the lower lip from corner to corner of the mouth.

Run a line from the corner of the mouth, down and around the jowl and up behind the nasal labial fold to the inside corner of the eye. Cut along the line with a 5 mm veiner.

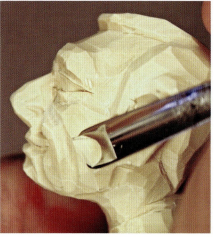

Cut under the cheekbone with a shallow gouge.

Separate the brow with a gouge.

Various views of the completed carving showing the final details. The carving is now ready to be finished.

Detail the hair of the brow with a 2 mm veiner.

Layout the hair track on the head. The direction runs forward from the part and then swings back.

After using a gouge to follow the hair track, remove a 3-corner chip from the top and bottom of the back of the ear to show the conical connection of the ear.

Begin the finishing process by coating the entire carving with boiled linseed oil. The oil will seal the wood and bring out the grain. I use a disposable foam brush to do this. Immediately wipe all the excess oil from the carving. Note that rags or paper towels that have been used with linseed oil can spontaneously combust and must be properly disposed of. Follow manufacturers warnings and directions.

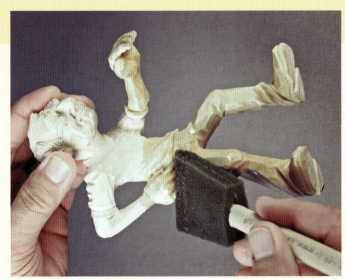

Coating with linseed oil.

The oiled carving can be sealed with a matte clear topcoat.

After sealing the carving, it is ready for paint. I use Americana acrylic paints. I begin by shading the cuts with burnt sienna to enhance the depth of the cuts. After shading, I apply thin washes of color until the desired effect is achieved. More shading is applied and a couple of light sprays with a matte clear topcoat finish the process.

Various views of the finished carving.

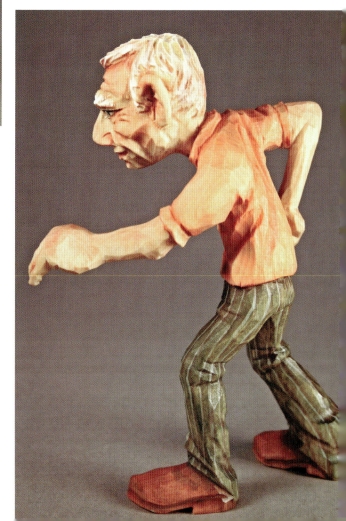

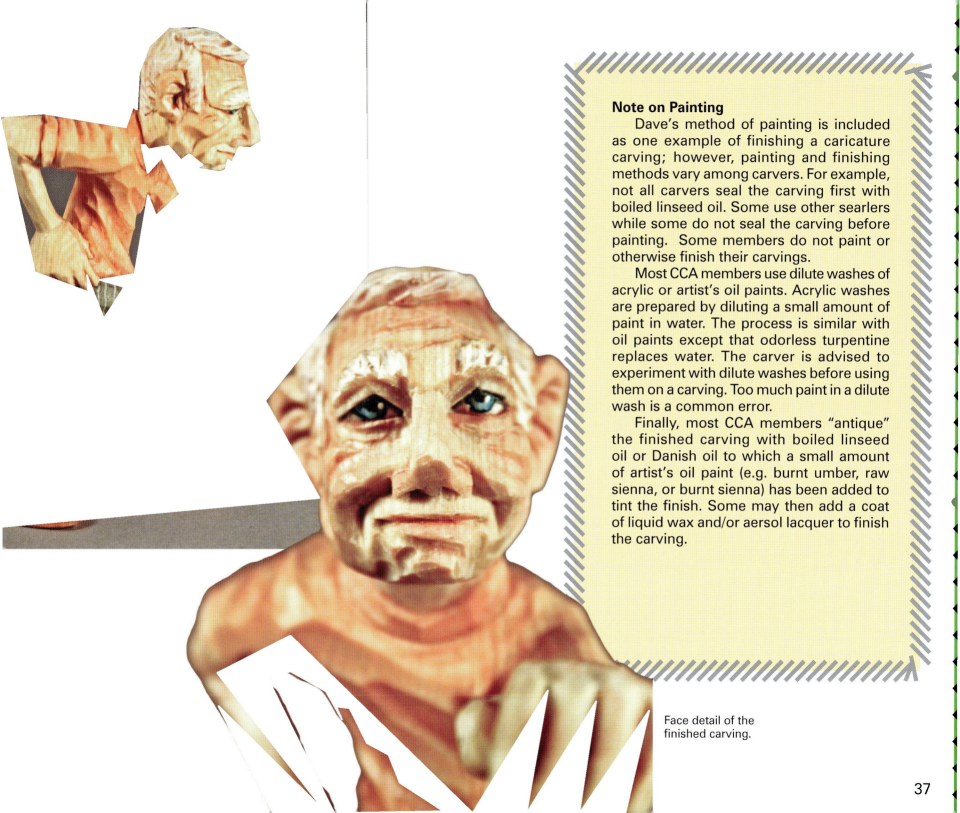

Note on Painting

Dave's method of painting is included as one example of finishing a caricature carving; however, painting and finishing methods vary among carvers. For example, not all carvers seal the carving first with boiled linseed oil. Some use other searlers while some do not seal the carving before painting. Some members do not paint or otherwise finish their carvings.

Most CCA members use dilute washes of acrylic or artist's oil paints. Acrylic washes are prepared by diluting a small amount of paint in water. The process is similar with oil paints except that odorless turpentine replaces water. The carver is advised to experiment with dilute washes before using them on a carving. Too much paint in a dilute wash is a common error.

Finally, most CCA members "antique" the finished carving with boiled linseed oil or Danish oil to which a small amount of artist's oil paint (e.g. burnt umber, raw sienna, or burnt sienna) has been added to tint the finish. Some may then add a coat of liquid wax and/or aersol lacquer to finish the carving.

Face detail of the finished carving.

THE CARVINGS & ACCESSORIES

Photos by Jack A. & Carole Williams

Rail Crossing Road

CCA

Tracks

DO NOT PUSH

Harley Schmitgen

Pete LeClair

Tom Brown

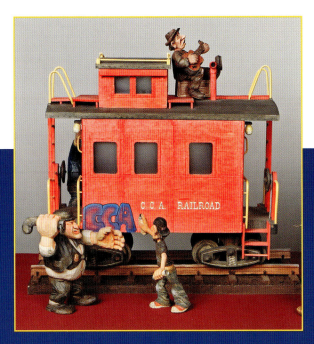

Gerald Sears

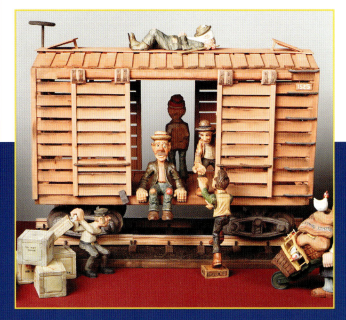

Cleve Taylor & Vic Otto

Dave Stetson

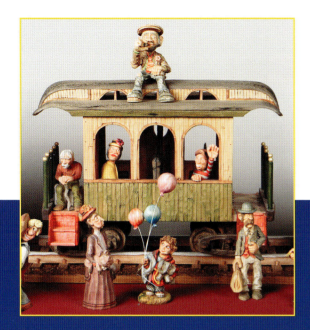

Gary Falin & Jack A. Williams

Doug Raine

Gary Batte

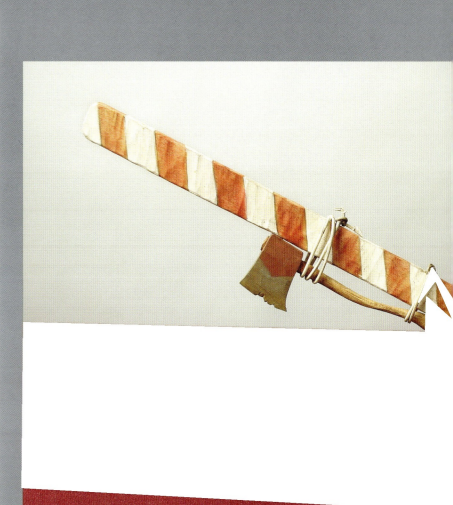

Phil Bishop

Phil Bishop

Phil Bishop

David Boone

Harold Enlow

Gary Falin

45

Desiree Hajny

Gene Fuller

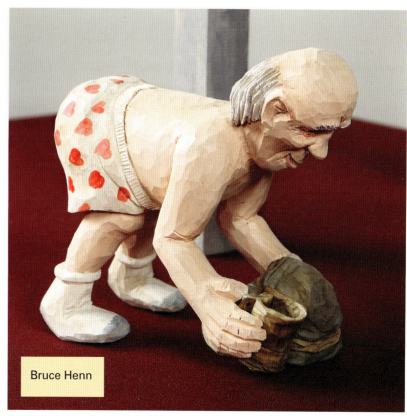

Bruce Henn

Will Hayden

Bruce Henn

47

Eldon Humphreys

Marv Kaisersatt

Marv Kaisersatt

Randy Landen

Pete LeClair

Pete LeClair

Keith Morrell

54

Keith Morrell

Cleve Taylor

Steve Prescott

Steve Prescott

Doug Raine

David Sabol

Floyd Rhadigan

Joe Schumacher

Dave Stetson

Dennis Thornton

Dennis Thornton

Dennis Thornton

Bob Travis

Tom Wolfe

Tom Wolfe

Woodcarving Demo Today!
HOBO CARVERS of AMERICA
presents featured carver
Karv Maisersatt

Joe You

Vic Otto

HEAD

front view   profile

HEAD

turned &
tilted back

©MARV KAISERSATT
2006

× 10"W.

NG TIES, RAILS, WHEELS & TRUCKS 15

BOX = 22"L × 17"W × 17"H.

NG BOX = 24"L × 19"W × 19"H.

OUTSIDE DIM.

CARVED FIGURES = 8" TALL.

PATTERNS*

Introduction

The patterns in this section were contributed by 20 CCA members. As you might imagine, there is considerable variation among members in the methods used to develop patterns. Some patterns are mere outlines of the finished carvings while others are drawn in considerable detail. Some show both front and side views, while others work from a single view. It should be noted that not all CCA members use patterns. Some, for example, work up a clay model for reference when doing the final carving. Others just draw a few lines on a piece of Basswood and begin carving. One member actually carves a miniature for use as a model. Still, others just pick up a piece of wood and begin carving. So, how did we obtain patterns for those pieces that were carved without patterns? There's no real secret here, the patterns were drawn after the carvings were completed.

The Steve Prescott Approach

Here is an example of how one member develops patterns. Steve began by simply listing some ideas for possible carvings. Included were a black porter, brakeman, conductor, engineer, fireman, fisherman, hunter, and passengers (military man, college student, boyfriend and girlfriend, business man, old maid, children, pets and other animals). Steve also considered such supporting objects as a dining car, line shack, mail car, Model T truck, tanker car, ticket office, and water tower. The boyfriend-girlfriend combination, the college student with megaphone, the man pulling the luggage cart, and the water tower were selected for further design. The man pulling the luggage cart and the water tower were discarded because other CCA members were doing similar carvings. The college student and the boyfriend-girlfriend ideas were discarded in favor of the final patterns noted below. However; we have included Steve's sketches on these ideas as examples of his approach.

*Note: All patterns are shown 50% of original size. For a full-size pattern enlarge 200%.

The Oiler and Conductor were the pieces that Steve decided upon for his contribution to the CCA Train. **Note:** Steve also carved the mother and child riding inside the passenger car; however, those patterns are not included here.

Some suggestions from Steve on developing patterns

Nearly all new carvers begin their carving careers by using patterns and projects designed by others. The CCA has always encouraged originality and creativity in its exhibitions and competitions. I am often asked, "How do you design a pattern?"

First, begin by modifying existing patterns. Trace the original, then move the arms and legs, or turn the head. These small variations will bring the confidence to design your own patterns.

The ability to draw is a real advantage, but not essential. Many CCA members carry a sketch pad and make small notes on interesting or humorous things they observe everyday. When sketching a new idea, don't worry too much about the detail, size or proportion; just get the general idea down. Write notes and ideas around the edge of the sketch. These ideas may or may not be used on the first carving, but may be used on later variations of that same pattern.

The final pattern (or band saw ready pattern) is drawn on Quadrille Grid graph paper. The front and side views are drawn side by side to keep both views proportionate. Don't worry about every little detail on the band saw pattern. Cut on the outside of the lines to give you a little more wood and more freedom to change the pattern if necessary.

Create a file for your patterns. This allows you to modify your patterns for future use just as you modified other patterns as a novice carver.

Other considerations on designing a pattern include:

1) Is the carving just for your enjoyment? If so, be as daring as you wish.

2) Will this be a class teaching project? If so, keep it simple unless you have only advanced students.

3) Is this to be a competition carving? If so, originality and uniqueness count!

4) Will this carving need to be shipped? If so, you may want to avoid fragile extensions that may break.

Brakeman oiling wheels

A Selection of Patterns from the CCA Train

Phil Bishop
Coolie

*Note: All patterns are shown 50% of original size.
For a full-size pattern enlarge 200%.

Gary Batte
Hobo with Cigar

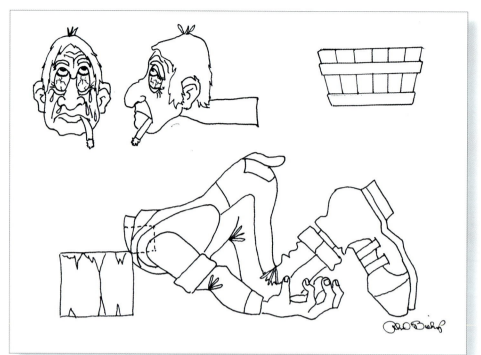

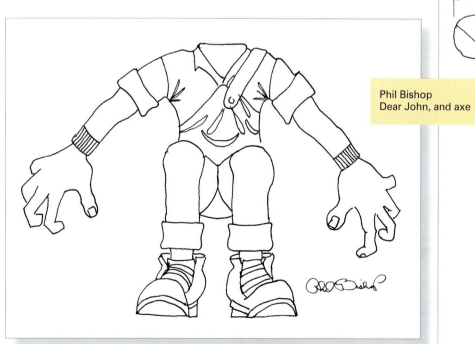

Phil Bishop
Dear John, and axe

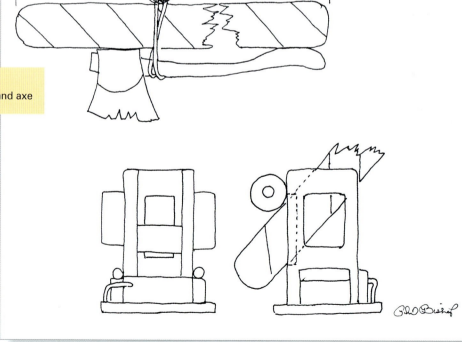

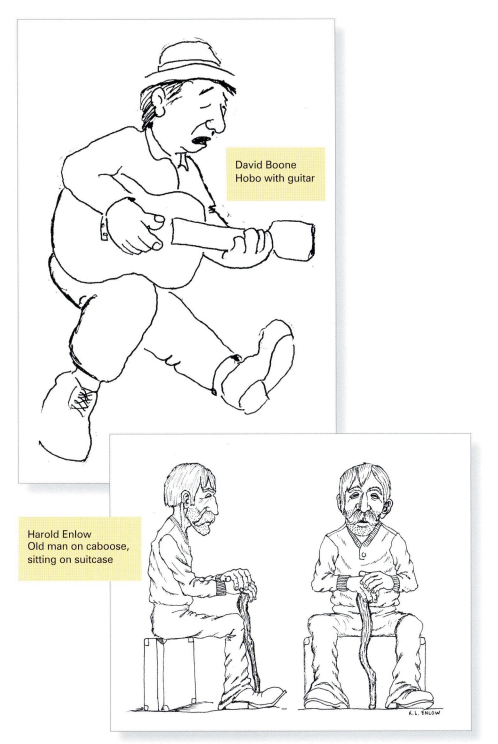

David Boone
Hobo with guitar

Harold Enlow
Old man on caboose,
sitting on suitcase

Gary Falin
Mechanic

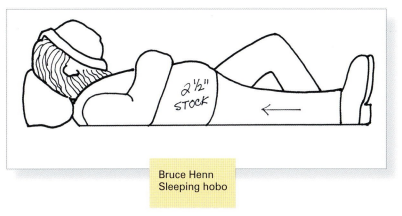

Bruce Henn
Sleeping hobo

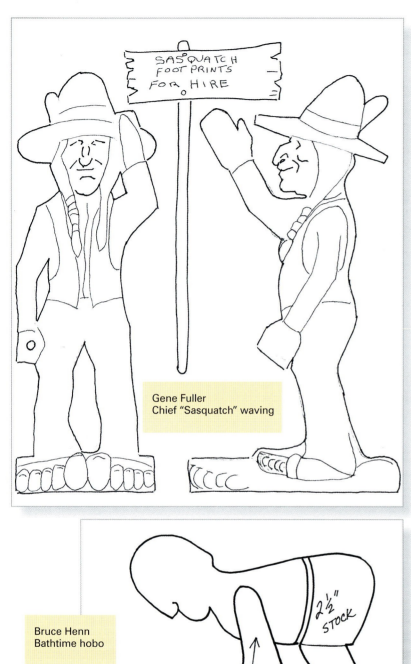

Gene Fuller
Chief "Sasquatch" waving

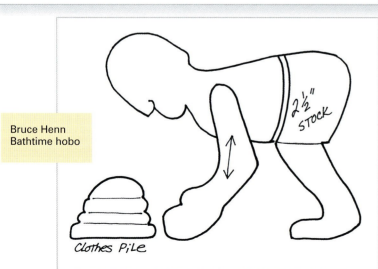

Bruce Henn
Bathtime hobo

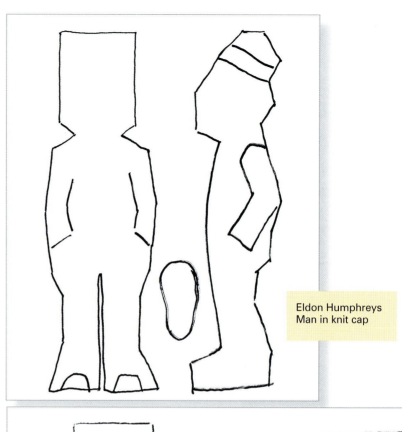

Eldon Humphreys
Man in knit cap

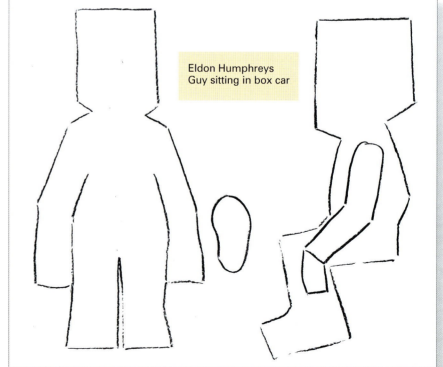

Eldon Humphreys
Guy sitting in box car

Marv Kaisersatt
Cow

Marv Kaisersatt
Lady with pig

*Note: All patterns are shown 50% of original size. For a full-size pattern enlarge 200%.

The Tagger
by Randy Landen

Randy Landen
Tagger

The Tagger
by Randy Landen

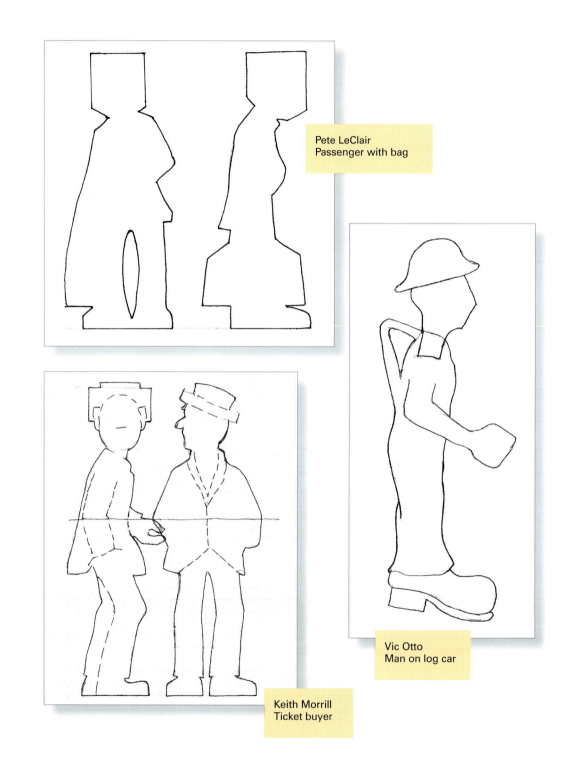

Pete LeClair
Passenger with bag

Keith Morrill
Ticket buyer

Vic Otto
Man on log car

76

Floyd Rhadigan
Indian man with pipe

Floyd Rhadigan
Indian woman with papoose and dog

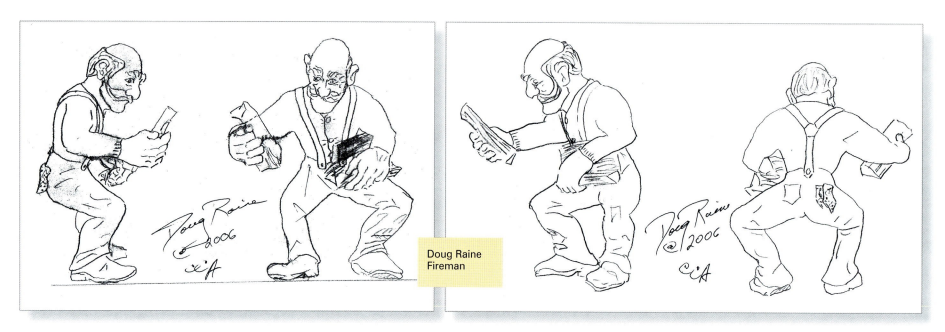

Doug Raine
Fireman

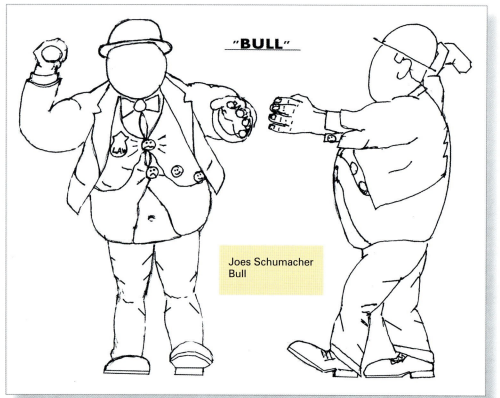

"BULL"

Joes Schumacher
Bull

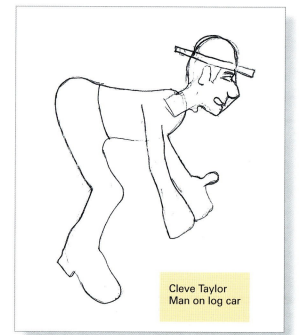

Cleve Taylor
Man on log car

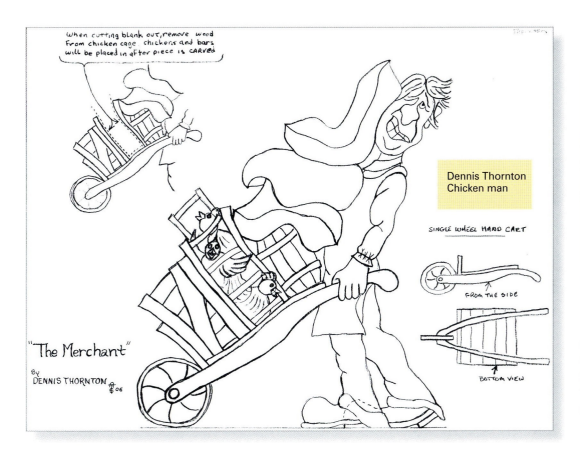

Dennis Thornton
Chicken man

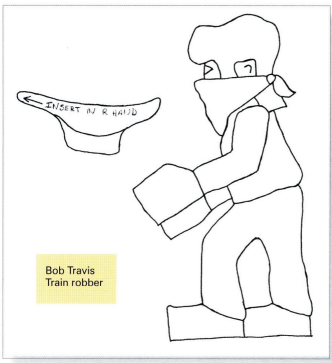

Bob Travis
Train robber

*Note: All patterns are shown 50% of original size. For a full-size pattern enlarge 200%.

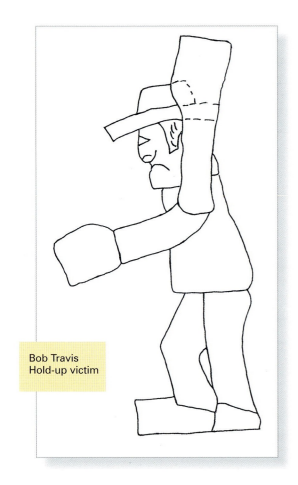

Bob Travis
Hold-up victim

Woodcarver - "Karv Maisersatt"

Joe You

Carver

Front

Carver

Side

Joe You
"Karv Maisersatt,"
carver

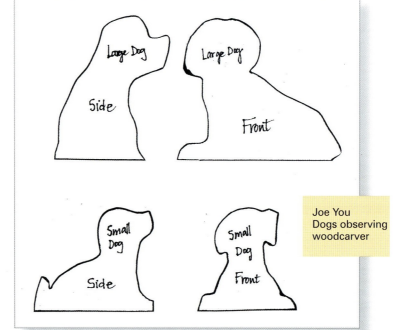

Large Dog

Large Dog

Side

Front

Small Dog

Side

Small Dog Front

Joe You
Dogs observing
woodcarver